SELECTED POEMS

Also by John Mole

The Love Horse
A Partial Light
Our Ship
From the House Opposite
Feeding the Lake
In and Out of the Apple
Homing
Depending on the Light

for children

Boo to a Goose
The Mad Parrot's Countdown
Catching the Spider
The Conjuror's Rabbit
Back by Midnight

criticism

Passing Judgements: Poetry in the Eighties

SELECTED POEMS

John Mole

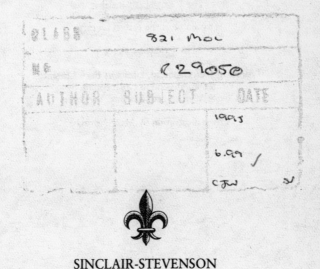
SINCLAIR-STEVENSON

The Selected Poems have been taken from the following publications:

The Love Horse (E J Morten, 1973)
A Partial Light (Dent, 1975)
Our Ship (Secker & Warburg, 1977)
From the House Opposite (Secker & Warburg, 1979)
Feeding the Lake (Secker & Warburg, 1981)
In and Out of the Apple (Secker & Warburg, 1984)
Homing (Secker & Warburg, 1987)
Depending on the Light (Peterloo Poets, 1993)

This collection first published in Great Britain in 1995
by Sinclair-Stevenson
an imprint of Reed Consumer Books Ltd
Michelin House, 81 Fulham Road, London SW3 6RB
and Auckland, Melbourne, Singapore and Toronto

A CIP catalogue record for this book
is available at the British Library

ISBN 1 85619 551 1

Typeset by Deltatype Ltd, Ellesmere Port, Cheshire
Printed and bound in Great Britain by
Cox & Wyman Ltd, Reading, Berkshire

Cover illustration by Mary Norman

To the memory of my father
Edgar Douglas Mole
(1910–1981)

Contents

from

The Love Horse (1973)

The Boy and the Sky

At his grandfather's house, at the top of the stairs
A small round window looked out on the sky;
It was empty, awful, a circle of nothing,
A transparent lid which blurred when the rain came
Or dazzled with sunlight, a frame but no picture;
It felt like a gap in the roof of his head,

And a curious buzzing began in his head
As he reached (past his bedtime) the foot of the stairs
Too afraid to go up; 'Oh you do look a picture'
His grandmother chuckled 'Afraid of the sky?
A brave boy like you?' Then his grandfather came
So he tried hard to tell him – got told it was nothing.

They didn't agree on the nature of nothing;
He couldn't explain; 'Don't go stuffing your head
With such nonsense' his grandfather ordered. 'You came
For a holiday. Buck up, enjoy yourself!' 'But it's the stairs,
It's the stairs!' he insisted 'They go to the sky
Through that window. There isn't a picture

Like downstairs.' He thought of the picture
He saw from the living room – that wasn't nothing
But something he knew about, putting the sky
In its place above landscape, a pattern, his head
Could make sense of it, not above stairs.
Again he looked up and the buzzing came

Louder, electric, like energy, came
And possessed him – the living-room picture
Clicked off and, abandoned, he charged up the stairs
Like a madman, his mind full of nothing,
Transparent and circular, threw back his head
As he ran and made mouths at the sky

While his grandparents watched him – 'It must be the sky.
Quick, the poor child's not well!' So the doctor came
Grumbling and made him say 'Ah', then he nodded his head
Saying 'Why did you bother me? This boy's the picture
Of health, he'll grow out of it. Really, it's nothing
But fantasy, just like The Man on the Stairs.'

'But it's *not*, it's the sky! There isn't a picture!'
The boy wept with rage when they came saying 'Nothing,
The doctor said', patted his head and went quietly
                                                    downstairs.

Two Painters

Picasso

Sometimes he painted birds. The boy stands
With a dove, warm in his gentle hands.

The boy grew. Always he painted man.
Some do as they must, some as they can . . .

A knock at his door – an officer
Come to inspect the studio finds Guernica

The blood, the paint still wet; 'Did
You do this, sir?' 'No, sir, you did.' . . .

Often, afterwards, he painted birds.
When I see them I think of those brave words,

Of the sharpening dark, a hooked cross,
And the dove ready – the albatross.

Paul Klee

Who lived

Whose cradled hieroglyphs
Made nursery walls of Time

Who spun his coloured toys
On chessboards or
The gyroscopic tensions of a graph

Whose grave face
Stared at us from exile
Darkened into history
Like Kafka's or Anne Frank's

Who wrote though
One day I shall lie down in
                    nothingness
Beside an angel of some kind

Whose child's eye
Ached for the child

Who died

Five Chantefables

(adapted from the French of Robert Desnos)

The Owls

The owls take a broad view:
some of them incline to
Plato, some to the new
learning – all eschew
what is suspect or untrue.

Mother owls make beau-
tiful mothers, a few
might brew more nourishing mouse stew
than they do
but most of them muddle through.

Owls' children do
as they are told, you
never get mumps or 'flu
if you're an owl-child, nor u-
sually does the cold turn you blue.

Owls, where do you
come from? What original venue?
A bamboo
hut? An igloo?
Are you Zulu,
Eskimo, or from Peru,
Timbuctoo, Anjou,
Andalu-
sia are you?

'Too-whoo! Too-whoo!'
they answer, 'it's too
bad, but we've forgotten if we ever knew.'

The Pelican

Captain Jonathan,
Eighteen and handsome,
Caught the first pelican
He could lay hands on,

But when Jonathan's pelican
Laid eggs for Jonathan
Out popped pelicans
Exactly like Jonathan's,

From which second pelicans'
Eggs laid for Jonathan
Out peeped a pelican
From the crack in each shell again . . .

Alas, poor Jonathan!

This could go on a long time
If you can't make omelettes.

The Zebra

The zebra is dark and pale.
Snug behind stripes
There are no escapes:
In gaol

Is a habit with him.
He is the doomed
Beast of his mind:
He would rush back in

If you let him out.
His prison
Warms him, freedom
Is not what he is about

Or the world . . .
An occasional dream
Now and then . . .
He sleeps curled

And his coat
Warms him – he bears
The print of his bars . . .

It is too late.

The Whale

Pity the poor whale –
She is nothing at all
But nostrils and an enormous lung.
She feeds cold milk to her young.
Nevertheless, piecemeal,
She builds a whale
Nest on the ocean bed
For each huge sleepyhead.
Beneath her move
Crustaceous depths, above
The celestial foam,
The wake of liners steaming home.

The Pike

The pike
Has journeys to make –
With a flick of his tail
He's off for the Nile
Or the Ganges
'Or' he says
'If I don't like either
There's the Tagus, the Tiber,
The Yangtze Kiang
Or . . .
What am I waiting for?'

Bursting with plans
He adjusts his fins.

And the moon, pike?
You could make it there too
Inside a week
Couldn't you?

Pike, I wish I had your go.

from

A Partial Light (1975)

The Roman Woman

This boy has broken from his friends, a busy
Party taking notes, to be alone with her —
Or with himself, my being here before him.

So we look down through the glass.
Her date's uncertain, vaguely Roman,
Part of these museum coins and brilliant tiles.

He watches her as if for movement.
Giving nothing back but silence
She invites me; cold, unfleshed,

The net we cast around this child
Is ruthless. Not a gladiator fighting
For his life could be more sudden or more cruel.

Heartless, her ribs maintain
Their brittle latticing, an architecture
Letting partial sunlight through

To keep it darkly. Bones
Cast from the feast are cast
In more perpetual shapes like this

And hint at some design I celebrate
By being here, by gazing back
Conspicuously dressed.

A cold exchange, her bright reflection
In the lake for glass to closet her.
That promise to each lover was a fiction.

3

The child's face boldly peering in
Imposes on her so she wears
His curious features like a patch of shroud.

The room grows dark around him.
Such a concentration holds him now,
That perfect skull and those extended fingers.

He is not mine. I move away
Past different curios, remembering
A cry that called me once past midnight

To my son's cot and the skeletal white bars
He clutched at, weeping there, as if
A heart had found its place and woken.

A Hereford Sampler

Sarah Bulmer, aged ten in 1835,
Stitched the name *Jesus* before all others.
This was, I imagine, an idea of her mother's
Or of *her* mother's who was doubtless alive

And very much so. If Sarah had friends
They were doing the same in similar homes –
Gratitude to Jesus was rife at that time
In embroidered script, each small hand

Led by the guiding hand. Poor Sarah –
She paused sometimes, her tight lips
Clenching the needle, thumbtip and fingertip
Runnelled with labour. Oh Sarah,

What pride when you finished? What duty
Done? Were you good then forever?
Stretched in its frame it doesn't look threadbare.
For what new task were you set free?

Whether for marriage or maidhood, I don't know.
These Hereford churchyards are weighty with stone.
Did you go far? I doubt it. If I left this room
And searched long enough I should probably find you.

Freud

'Tell me your dream' said Freud
thoughtfully
sucking his pencil.

'If you tell me yours, then' said the patient
petulantly
sucking her thumb.

'In my dream' said Freud
thoughtfully
'you are sucking your thumb
and being petulant.'

'Likewise' said the patient
petulantly
'in my dream you are sucking your pencil
and being thoughtful.'

'You are standing naked
in a Leonardo landscape' Freud added
(making it sound like an afterthought)
'but you are innocent
hence the thumb.'

'And you are sitting
very close' continued the patient
'so close it rather frightens me
but you are only making thoughtful sketches
hence the pencil.'

'Come, you are imagining things'
said Freud

petulantly.

'Which is why I am here'
said the patient

thoughtfully.

Songs for an Abandoned Car

1

Lie still, lie still, it all
Goes on without you
Somewhere behind another wheel
But in the same direction.

Rest, though not quite done
With never quite life —
Propped, wide-eyed
Almost skull with one door open
Like an ear listening.

2

So what do you hear?
A whisper of destinations
In the radial's tread?
So what do you hear?
A speed buffeting the wind?

Yes, and a smaller sound
Like grass, almost.
Somewhere beyond this
A man walks upright.

Waking Early

Already the first touch
Is mirrors, windows –
Outside, a dark tree
Spreads on our quilt of panes.
It waves like Ophelia . . .

And glass is heavier than air
And breakable as water.
Only in sleep we sink a little
Without drowning, the frail blood
Locked in our wrists forever.

Last Touch

One finger crossing my palm –
I hold you there . . .

This is our last touch
Before sleep, a small weight's

Heavy promise, flesh-tip
Bedded in loss.

When it leaves,
Your absence presses home.

from

Our Ship (1977)

The Toy Piano

The mouth of the toy piano
grits its teeth. It bites
habitually on mice and teddy-bears
but is dissatisfied.

The wired belly tinkles
for stronger meat,
those harmonies of suffering
beyond the cradle.

Branches of dark forests
where each bird has earned its song
enchant the piano.
Only what hurts matters

and this child will matter
when he is not a child.
But while they play together
in a lighted room

the piano hates him.

Con Amore

She practises the clarinet,
Her back turned to a spacious window.

No sound reaches the garden.
Music, on a stalk of silence,

Waves behind glass.
She turns her own pages.

Phrase by phrase
The theme is movement only

As the flowers all know
Inclined towards her.

Love must blossom on its stalk
Before she hears it,

And the pages turn
Like a white rose opening.

Looking at Daffodils, in the Old Fashion

Their fierce display was current briefly:
Crisp on its stalk, each golden horn
Is paper-money now. What reason
For such innocent and natural treason?
Who bought whom? To be unborn
And not betrayed to death! But chiefly

This: that what is left may buy
Something back still from so much taken –
Neither to haggle at the price
Nor wait for sensible, informed advice
But *now*. Before the last is shaken
Earthwards. Not to know how, yet try.

The Punch Family

I was much affected by the internal troubles of the Punch family. I
thought that with a little more tact on the part of Mrs Punch and
some restraint held over a temper, naturally violent, by Mr Punch,
a great deal of this sad misunderstanding might have been
prevented.

Edmund Gosse, Father and Son

He was always alone in this:
Each holiday, with seaside friends
Who weren't his friends, he gazed
At a high tent's awful hole
And shuddered. Something amiss,
Unnameable, a huge stick
Pummelling his shapeless soul
Like pastry. Even the jolly stripes
Reminded him of blood. Amazed,
Not as a child is by some party trick,
He learned from squeaking archetypes
The terror on which life depends.

And later, back at the grim hotel
Which never let him out of sight
But set a righteous face against the sea
In red-bricked anger, echoes
Put on flesh; *Your mother isn't well . . .
This place . . . the air . . .* His father's voice
Was hard like making deals. *She chose
To rest a little on her own this afternoon.
I had a word with them. They sent up tea.
I don't know why we come here. It's her choice.*
Something was still unnameable but soon
That show, too, finished for the night.

At breakfast, nothing made sense.
Once more the same pain
Shuddered across the table as they thrust

26

Their glumness at each other. Why?
What huge stick in the silence
Hung above them? When would it hammer down
And end this? When would she cry
Or he be gone forever?
                              So, each holiday
Each morning, always, one small boy must
Leave them alone in this, a fixed frown
Souring his heart, and, friendless, go and play
With friends, and in the evening come again.

The Boy Guru

Scene: a delicatessen
in Luton. Cast: solo.
It's the ghost of the Boy Guru's
poster again

outfacing price
reductions, taped to the window –
Green peppers, garlic, no
parmesan today, and *Peace! Peace!*

Not the moon but
cream floating on coffee;
an affluent simile
for a sect

made in our image.
Features of foie gras
(all faith is grass),
we guess at his age –

fourteen? Already
round his head
the blue has faded.
Somewhere in the sky

beyond sight
a throb of engines –
He has taken our sins;
he's flown out.

The Fair

Welcome they say

By kind permission of the mayor
Your town will wake tonight.

Our quoits fall short.
We choke a duck
With ping-pong balls.

Behind each dodgem's
Painted snarl, a father
Steering recklessly, one-handed,
As he hugs his son.

A pair of dark arms
Lock at midnight, reaching
For the height from which we fell.

The corporation flower-bed
Is a bearded lady.

Laws are passed.

Notes for a Talking Head

Introduced. Stand.
Thank variously. Acknowledge
applause if any.
If none make joke get laugh
however (Topical?
Local ref? Vicar? Rush-hour
if heavy indust.?)
Adjust mic. if mic./
'Can you hear at back?'
if village hall etc.
'That better?'
Begin.

Quote hand-out
'Everything in my power will be done
by the party I represent
to represent you in everything
the party has done.'
This obvious.
Needless to say
time is now. Only
coward running looks behind.
Are on the move.
Past must take care of self.
Personal note: don't own
own house. Know to be others
in own position (pause)
or worse (long pause).
Quote hand-out
'None shall go empty.'
Be seeing to that as far
as can as in me lies
to change the course of things.
Prices high as beanstalk.
Am no giant-killer but try.
This little/important spot/area

forever England where I
speak to you today
of years to come and many
on the bright side too.
Remember your voice always
my voice. Never too busy etc.
People my business.
As for threatened motorway
and education have myself
car and three plus new arrival
children. Deplore as much as you do.

End. Sit.
Fumble a bit
with papers etc.
Pour glass of water.
Pour glass of water for chairman
if lady. If any
applaud other speakers.
Keep smiling.

Paterfamilias

A ravished bride and her abundant progeny
Sit round the table, mirrored in mahogany.

Which of the children have their father's face?
The eldest son recites a Latin grace.

Enter Jessie from the Servants' Quarters.
Marcus is in love with both her daughters.

Cecil's ambitious; his amours are Gallic.
Ralph finds the pepper-pot distinctly phallic.

Jessie brings a dish and lifts its lid;
Monica has told her what Hugh did

But she herself has always fancied John —
One needs the sweetmeats when one's tooth is long.

Gertrude is senior on the distaff side;
She's been an angel since her father died.

Sarah reads novels; such a pity she
Cannot make sense of sensibility.

Annette likes stories from the underworld;
Inside her velvet shoes her toes are curled.

Which leaves plain Jane, her mother's greatest joy
Despite some trouble with the gardener's boy.

The portrait on the blue-veined mantelpiece
Of course is Father, prior to his decease.

A pair of urns, Victorian-Hellenic
(Ralph declares that they're distinctly phallic)

Flank the gilded frame on either hand.
Ralph was the son he tried to understand.

His ideal was Arcadian – a chaste
Unravished bride of quietness and taste

Depicted palely on a brittle surface.
Searching in every child of his for her face

He found, alas, another and another
Resolute facsimile of its mother.

Now they sit, without him, round the table
Fleshing out a Great Victorian Fable,

Demonstrating sadly how it feels
To be the sediment of High Ideals,

An odd, bewildered human residue –
Five boys: John, Marcus, Cecil, Ralph and Hugh,

Their sisters and their mother. What a life!
So much depends on choosing the right wife.

A Proper Caution

When Grandpa on my mother's side,
The playful one, rolled up his sleeves
And tap-danced at the carpet's edge
At tea-time, as he often did,
His second wife was not amused –
How strangely Arthur still behaves!
Embarrassed by his flashing shoes,
She frowned as if she'd signed the pledge.

So when a vagueness called The Arts
Became the thing for me to do
And not my father's father's firm
Which claimed my father, it was said
Poor Arthur's silly fits and starts
Are coming out in John. They knew
Exactly where I'd got it from –
To put such ideas in his head!

But what they never knew was this –
The time when, at his study desk,
He showed me with such seriousness
How business letters should be brisk
And always end Yours Faithfully
Then smiled, as from the living-room
Came *Arthur! Don't you want your tea?* . . .

He didn't dance that afternoon.

The Wordsworth Concordance

Less than two hundred references to *Child*.
Innocence, surprisingly, rates ninety-three.
Was he not what we thought he was? Compiled
At length at Cornell University
It should be accurate enough, yet *Birth*
Still gets a meagre eighty-seven's worth.

Try *Death*. One hundred and ninety various deaths –
Mere marginal improvement there. And *Dead*?
Not often. The Romantic shibboleths
Disport themselves most dismally. Instead,
We might as well spend no more wasteful time,
Settling for *Nothing* with its ninety-nine.

But what's this list, five solid pages long?
Yes, yes. Of course. The complement to *Dove*,
Where heaven is, than whom more truly strong?,
Etcetera, etcetera. O LOVE,
You clear a clean eight hundred, give or take,
And Poetry's back in business, no mistake!

Emily Dickinson was Right about This

Art she wrote *is a house*
Which tries to be haunted.
Always the same choice –
Wake the dead
Or pack up and go.
Art is Yes or No.

Even after a lifetime
To move out, admit
The place was fine,
I liked it
But who came there?
Staying is nowhere.

Yet all of us stay
Or, at least, most.
Who dare say
They have seen no ghost
And never will?
Truth can kill.

Safer, by far, to wait
In a pleasant room,
Plan, decorate –
It must happen soon.
Get off to a good start,
Patience is an art.

Off the Hook

So many hands reach out for them
and leave them standing;
office telephones – *Hello?* –
A new girl paints her nails.

They bark at their reflections
in the cold formica –
Hello, Hello, Hello . . .
To each its empty cradle.

Someone has gone for someone
everywhere. Ubiquitous glass
dispenses sunlight to a vacancy
of table-tops and chairs.

Alas, the tiny voices!
These are the lost, the hopeful,
trapped in a mouthpiece
waiting to be put through.

One by one, they die
at the end of patience –
a perspective of upturned turtles
on Christmas Island.

Six o'clock encroaches
and the tide is roaring.
No one will come now.
Even the sun goes home.

Looking Like Rain

A sullen darkening around our faces
holds us apart. Once more, the world
moves in on itself and it looks like rain.

After, there are no words for what rain looked like;
only for how, with a new brightness,
the air heals behind what has passed through.

From the House Opposite

1

Our bed heaves slowly with its strange
unsettled load, a moisture
this side of the window proving
we were here if proof they need
who see so eye to eye it seems
their blind hides nothing.

2

So, once more, we're woken by
their children running in
our corridors, and it's as if
they almost felt at home until
a sudden, fearful Mummy! Daddy!
echoes wrongly, out of place.

3

It's good to find warm toast
on all our plates, a frieze of smiles
around the happy tables and
a vapour wrapping us,
but who has made this meal?
Could it be theirs we eat?

4

They watch us leave together
with the children, still not ours
exactly though they make no move
to claim them. A conspiracy
has let us kidnap two small orphans
and no punishment will fit this crime.

5

From what we were the house
discharges us. Three empty bottles

glisten on the doorstep
like a token of good faith,
and someone's cat is settling in the window
waiting for whoever may come home.

Her Song

Dear Mickey Mouse, our wires have crossed
Because too long my heart was set
Upon a limber marionette
And only came to you when lost.

Oh stronger men in sharper suits
Have swept me from the bustling floor
But still, my love, how I adore
Those tiny yellow plastic boots.

Too late, too late to burn your ears
With talk about you now you're gone.
I feel my headache coming on,
The throbbing which must end in tears.

But while your mischief fills the screen
I stretch towards you for a kiss
Then falter, 'What's the point of this?'
His children wonder what I mean.

Supposing, love, they had been yours,
A little mine but oh your nose and
Yip yip Yankee lederhosen —
Just my smile, perhaps, no more.

The sun sets as you skip away,
The circle closes to a dot,
Their father likes his supper hot . . .
I've hardly thought of him all day.

And so she sang, as one half dead
Alleviates the afternoon,
Because she knew that someone soon
Would help her gently back to bed.

The Tales of Rover

108 prizes for obedience

Rover, of these the proud possessor,
looks you squarely in the eye, unblinking.

His coat is sleek with ineffable goodness.
Stroke it. Feel how it helps your hand across.

You dream, perhaps, of walking on the water?
Yes, he could even do that if he tried.

He says: *We could all do that if we tried.
If brilliance and virtue went together.*

The dog it was survived

Mr and Mrs Prince don't like each other.
Rover, lately, has not liked them either.

Something in their voices when they say 'Good boy'
appalls him, and the children oh the children

they grew up and left. He loved them
but they'll come no more, and now the bones oh

now the bones he buries are the Princes
lodged together where they won't be found.

Rover considers an exemplar

Little he cared for stories in his puppyhood
despite the many books about a special Rover

who, he recalls, walked proudly upright,
put a waistcoat on and changed his name.

Apotheosis of the self-made hound
in appetising plates. O glittering fob-watch!

Moral tales says Rover *for the little Princes.*
Dogs have ambitions but mine are not those.

What makes it worse

The Black Dog oftentimes sore troubleth Rover.
Stretched on the Chesterfield they groan together,

practised companions of the mordant phrase
which bites life to the bone then worries it.

Sometimes the erudition of their stichomythia
redeems an hour or two, until at last

repentant Rover cries: *Enough! Avaunt!*
and finds himself alone though none the happier.

He contemplates a Great Adventure

Cutlass between his teeth, and hideous eye-patch,
Peg-leg Rover leaps from the stockade.

He has chewed up a map of Treasure Island.
Well, it seemed the answer. They were far too greedy.

Gold. If he hears that word again, he says . . .
He says: *I've spent a life-time holding off the Princes.*

Now just a stretch of sand across the water
then a sail will blossom and its bones be crossed.

Rover sidesteps an important issue

Rover is asked for his World-view.
Is man a wolf to man in puppy's clothing?

He says: *I do not hold opinions.*
They are accursed. I could describe the Princes.

People who look about, who sigh, who say
'It's a dog's life' and seem to mean it;

people who might have had a very special bone,
whose god has buried it but is not telling.

An affair of the heart

Yesterday, the Princes bought a book;
its title, *Caring for your Pet*, amuses Rover.

Dogs above all, the author says, respond to you.
Says Rover: *Marvellous. So now they tell me.*

He has seen gerbils fretting at their cage —
the pepper-corn eyes, the rancid sawdust —

yet it was him the Princes had to choose.
A civilized lifetime petted without love.

He seeks a virtue in decorum

Rover treads softly on the path of love.
Affections come and go, a vanishing perspective.

Always he justifies the ways of dog to man
and seldom makes the two-backed beast in public.

Passionate? *Well, yes* he says *I can be.*
Lust has its moments in my repertoire

but sentiment's a matter for discretion.
One cannot be too careful about this.

He nearly forgets himself

Rover's effervescent blood in springtime
sparkles to the tip of each keen paw.

He races out across the lawn. He gambols.
Blossom lures him from his ancient ways.

The bones, he cries, *the bones! They push up daisies.*
Where oh where the hands that made the chains?

Alas, departed with the Princes' children.
Rover, even now, surrenders to his grief.

Rover's global awareness

Whenever Rover glances at the News
he finds a world which vindicates the Princes.

Dog eats dog, they say he says.
If we went on like this, there'd soon be changes.

Earnest endeavours of important men
whom no one trusts because they look so lonely . . .

Rover's alarmed about the world's resources.
Government should be a limited supply of bones.

An interim report

Things are getting worse now with the Princes.
No one visits them. *Would you?* asks Rover.

Shrill grows the desperate voice of Mrs Prince
when dust collects in her remotest corners.

'Next to Godliness!' she cries. 'Remember that!' –
'Oh carry me out in a box!' implores her husband.

Rover says: *At least I have my basket*
and they still say Good dog if I keep it clean.

He defines the necessary limits

Rover deplores the Baron Frankenstein
and all who won't accept the terms of Nature.

Mongers of immortality; grotesque illusion.
Bones are bones he says *and there an end*.

Thy soul shall be required of thee, so keep it kennelled.
Groom it, never let it out at night

and don't deny the god beneath your skin.
Insane ambition meets with just deserts.

Rover draws to a close

When beggars die there are no comets seen.
No heavens blaze forth the death of Princes.

Or of dogs, adds Rover. *We deserve,*
the lot of us, precisely what we get.

He says: *A bone, a basket, and tomorrow.*
Ownership may pass from man to man

but someone loves us sometime if we're lucky.
All is not lost because the cupboard's bare.

Rover among the angels

Thou wast not made for death, immortal dog!
We hail the superhound, our last romantic.

In his dreams, become a winged avenger,
Rover wheels above the darkening flood.

Behold him, shades of Kierkegaard and Nietzsche;
how he sparkles with ethereal moisture

then awakes, a slipper in his mouth,
and settles gently at his Master's feet.

The Question

Je est un autre
Rimbaud

So I asked: is there only
this place? And if so
which wall should he stand
with his back to, presuming
the choice must be mine?

But they said: through that window
all doubts are resolved
if you wish (if he trusts us enough)
so I jumped and, still asking,
arrived at this place.

The Lord

Everything in my aunt's life Was To Be
in everybody's life, especially ours. The Lord
would see to that all right. The sudden rain
which spoiled a picnic, skies of unbroken blue
next day – all bearable pain,
all love, was His. None, she said, could afford
to hide from Him, to whom were due
submission, praise, and a fearsome glory.

Praise Him, therefore, for such fearsome glory
as my aunt submitted to. Her due
in times when she could ill afford
to give it heed was pain until she died, a pain
which seemed just bearable. Skies of unbroken blue
broke over her, and sudden rain
in everybody's life, especially hers. The Lord
had seen to that all right. It Was To Be.

Mr Tod

Mr Tod, sartorial
in Brummell splendour,
takes our admiration
as a fox's due.

'Good sir, kind sir,
pray who is your tailor?
Whence the buckled shoes
and cherry waistcoat?

Such a handsome cane
of ebony and silver;
how the gloss beguiles us
on your elegant black hat!'

Says he, 'Of course,
why ever not, dear children?
I have always done my best
to make things pleasant.

Let the inescapable
observe decorum,
let the scent of death be sweet,
its texture satin.'

Gracious Mr Tod
whose style means business,
picking feathers from his teeth
and sweeping clean.

The Garden

1

A sampler of daisies
Unstitched by the children.
Chains for her neck
To wear until evening.

Bedtime. *Goodnight Dad*
Before the light goes.
Blades at dusk. A world
Clean-shaven when they wake.

2

The garden pocketed
And played for trumps;
You should see my lawn.
It took us years.

The children pocketed
In costly schools.
She sends them photographs —
Your father's well.

3

Age comes like this:
I'm worried about the grass,
A smaller place . . .
But she'll never go.

Chains for her neck
On summer afternoons,
A grandchild's small fists
Clutching daisies.

4

It took years
And the years have taken –
Two closed deck-chairs
On a cold veranda.

So, another couple
From persuasive agents –
She likes the house. He says
The garden will need work.

The Forest

Sweetmeats, and a horror
in each twist of tree bark;
Gingerbread Gingerbread
cry the Rackham faces

and another face, another
in the leafless branches grinning
Never Never. No one told you
about this.

You came here innocently
with your sister. Now
you cling together, huddled
underneath a tree.

Nightfall is a huge mouth
opening to eat you –
No, you are not dreaming.
You are here.

Silence at first
becoming birdsong. Dawn
reveals one tenuous remaining
face above you; then

a sudden soft thud
in the leaf-mould
and a voice is crying
Home. Come home.

So, hand in hand
you leave the forest;
slowly, a dark book,
it closes behind you.

Mother! Father!
Such a welcoming –
Their faces in the doorway
hang like fruit.

Bestial Homilies

Darwin's Ape weeps underneath a tree—
Further, my God, than ever and ever from Thee.

Lear's Owl is singing to his small guitar—
Love is a pussy. What beautiful pussies there are.

Carroll's White Rabbit hasn't made it yet—
He drops in at the lab for one last cigarette.

Tennyson's Eagle plummeting from his crag—
The world belongs now to the cormorant and shag.

Melville's Whale, a transatlantic freak—
Out of the mouths of babes . . . and even dolphins speak.

Somebody's faithful dog, no matter whose—
Good dogs are always faithful. Treacherous ones make news.

My cat purrs loudly through the bulletins—
Her aerial whiskers twitch, indifferent to our sins.

Behold, a tiny autocratic mouse—
He's thinking big. He plans to overthrow the house.

Be warned by Nature not to let things go—
The beasts prepare to say: We told you so.

Snowfall

It came late,
Filling the garden,
Feathering the gate,

And blown through the door
A few flakes'
Reminiscent pallor

Smudging your toes
Then gone . . .
A surreptitious

Trick of vanishing
As if two hearts
Might still take wing.

A Carol

Absolute naked little head, beginner,
how you leap once more from darkness
like your word against another, first
at everything, a busybody
starting out in life, so eager —

May you blaze and blaze forever
as our world shrinks older, colder
to a bitter star —
O Innocent, reproachful one,
we need your helpless light.

Easter Gifts

Blood from a stone,
Water from rock,
Bread from the bone,
Sing Giant, sing Jack.

Wine from water,
Bone from the flood,
Stone from the cave-mouth,
Sing Bread, sing Blood.

Rocks for the Giant,
Water for Jack,
A song for us all,
Sing Love, sing Lack.

from

Feeding the Lake (1981)

Love

This is a word intact. The century
Has smuggled it into our keeping.
We have built it a shelter
Among ashes, marked with a cross.

How it survived its passport
Baffles us. We ask no
Questions. We suffer its hurt look.
It deserves peace.

Gently between our joined hands
It pulses, gently becomes
The light of our gaze across a landscape
At the cold dust endlessly rising.

The Double Agent

Your announcement of his birth takes up two pages
Of the latest double issue, and a double album
Sings his praises to the world. Immediately
All lucky numbers double at the joyful news
Old Double's dead and that his son New Double
Is the Double of his Dad, and very soon he's after
Double value as you wheel his double push-chair down
                                         perspectives
Double-wrapped for freshness, seeing double,
To the girl whose double, yesterday, rang up
Her double figures and whose double-cross

Is double negative, the not the not
Of what you do not need, the double knot
Which presses on your neck, the hangman's double
Certainty, the double-dealing of the doubled-up
Smart operator laughing while his double time
Is served by others, whose indemnity comes
Doubled and whose double shakes your hand and bids you
Doubly welcome, promising redoubled efforts
On your own behalf, a careful balancing
Of double columns doubling your chances,

But remember: once you were single-hearted
In your love of singleness, a single ticket took you
Anywhere you wanted. One by one by one
The stops defined your journey, each one singly
Pressing at the window with imponderable purpose
Singling you out. You were the singleton, the only,
Child of original desire and certitude, the sole
Redemptive image whose reflection was
Yourself alone. But now? . . . Oh more than ever
I'm in love with you and could not hurt a single hair.

The Journey

His lost face travels with him on the glass
Deep into tunnels he has never dared to name,
Ignites explosive sunlight, cries *Alas*,
Then finds another landscape where those same
Abandoned features peer back through broad day,
Reprint indifference, give no game away.

The carriage speeds on smoothly over tracks
Worn whistle-clean, punctilious. He tries
To sit back, plan adventures and relax,
Allowed some larger scene to monarchise,
But always, like a half-developed plate,
That ghost reproaches him: *Too late, too late.*

Out there the grass grows wilder, water shines
From tense horizons twilight sets on edge;
He gazes boldly now, his heart inclines
To feel it might still dare — self-knowledge
Would not come before, but face to face
He'll move towards the window just in case.

Then, as he takes each step, such darkness fills
The space behind him that there seems no choice;
A final landscape beckons and distils
Essential emptiness into a voice —
At last! it cries; he sees no face appear,
And crying too *At last, at last!* leaps clear.

The Skill

What's left but the skill?
I float on a rhyme
And am half asleep.
Though these waters shine
They are not still
Nor do they run deep.

You have taken the sense
From all that I seemed to know—
Soon, on a dry bed,
I shall dream the slow
Deceptive confluence
By which our lake was fed.

Park Ducks

From the lake's rim
They peck at transistors,
Pampered daily
By the food of love.

Around their world
Go the striped push-chairs –
A small child leads them
With his trumpeting cone.

Who is without sin
Or bread? At dusk
The moon is vanilla.
The gates close.

It can't be stones
We cast on the water –
Each bright slice
Blooms where it fell.

Across the Lawn

Long, long the lemon in tall glasses
And the sad attenuated legs of Strachey
In Lamb's portrait, and the books
Too many of them really and too long.

And long, long the palisades, the privet
And the acid conversation, and the sets
In friendly matches, and the silly silly war
Which really has been going on too long.

Oh long, long the living of this life
Too long, an equilibrium of stone and stone
In walking finally across the lawn
Towards kind water which has waited long.

Nocturne

— A version of Mallarmé's *Brise Marine*

Utterly tired, and all our good books read,
I gaze out on the ocean. Overhead
Across the darkness spilling from my eyes
The sharp gulls trace familiar surprise
Then leave it vacant. Nothing here for me
Except this dull absorption by the sea,
More empty paper and a bland desk-light.
I've watched you feed our child without delight . . .
Oh more, much more! How very small love is,
Diminished further by the destinies
We shaped once for each other. No farewell
Would leave us elsewhere than as now in hell
Or happier than huge rocks in storm
Inviting shipwreck, envious of each torn-
To-tatters masthead. So we stay, we stay,
While slowly one more night drifts onto day
And anchors safely. Tell me what went wrong . . .
I hear, but cannot write, the ocean's song.

Conversation Pieces

Schubert and Candles

'Yes, I'll stay,' she agreed, 'I mean, seeing you've laid out the
                                                                table
But that'll be it, absolutely, compris, just the meal
And some brief conversation for afters. You're pretty
                                                        unbearable
Aren't you – all Schubert and candles, my darling, and "How
                                                        do you feel
About us?" Well, I don't, though it never seems right at the
                                                                time
To say *how* much I don't, and especially through there – in the
                                                                bed –
Where I'm laid like a table – Oh Christ, what's the difference! –
                                                        the wine
Turning bitter and stale on our breath as you slice up my
                                                        bread.'

So she stayed, yes, and so did the candles – unlit – and no
                                                        music,
And all the meal long he said nothing except what he had to
Like 'Is it all right?' – so subdued she expected some trick
Up his sleeve or up something at least, yet was curiously glad to
Feel nothing when, gently, his face buried deep in her hair,
She found she was kissing his fingers, then crying, then going
                                                        through there.

Probably Not

'We should try it this time,' she suggested, 'yes, really.'
'On the whole, no,' he replied. 'I think probably not.
Look, I'm thirty-nine now and I've just about reckoned what's
                                                                what
And what isn't. *This* isn't (it could have been once) quite for
                                                                me.'
'Bullshit,' she countered, and countered so sweetly,
So young, so determined, unsmiling, he almost forgot

70

Who she was, and who he was, all caution, discretion, the lot
Swept away in an instant, amazing her, leaving him free.

What a word can achieve, though, one more, be it known, can
                                                        undo.
'Well, *perhaps*,' he conceded, 'but shouldn't we, as it were,
                                                        wait?'
'Oh Jesus!' was all she could manage. 'Oh hey nonny no!'
'And that's just what I thought you would say,' he said,
                                        'something like that.'
So again it was over, as usual, was over, but 'See you,'
They said when they parted, not coldly, as if they still might.

Passing North

'My God, is it you?' he exclaimed, as she stood in the doorway
Not looking at him but the Cotman they'd bought after
                                                    Norwich
And she didn't take though he'd offered. 'I mean, can you stay?
Would you like to? How long? Why? Who are you with? Which
Hotel? . . .' and she still wasn't looking at him but the love-
                                                    spoon
They'd picked up in Wales the next day and she hadn't packed
                                                    either
But coveted now, just a little, this cold afternoon
Passing north on her own – well, who bothered? – to live there
                                                    or die there.

He could have said more to the point like 'Why didn't you
                                                    write?'
But he didn't, and what was the point of it now? After all
It was years since he'd thought of her much, bless her heart; out
                                                    of sight
Out of mind. Oh, that painting? That spoon? Absorbed by the
                                                    wall –
How seldom he noticed them, then he did notice – at last – it
                                                    was him
She was looking at, smiling a little: 'Well, shall I come in?'

What Dreams May Come

The platform is softly lit
For my arrival. As I approach,
An old benevolence shines on the tracks.

Every sign says *Home*.
There is bunting on the signals.
A light winks in its little box.

Somewhere the band, as it must,
Goes *oompah*, somewhere
A high voice cries for comfort

But my father has turned
And is walking away. It seems
He has mistaken the time. I call out

As he disappears, his tired smile
Facing the darkness. What awaits us both
Is the point of our departures,

Separation, loss, beneath a luminous
Clock's cream face and the moon
Possessed of its milky secret.

Ballroom Dancers

If music has an edge
They catch its meaning
And their formal pattern
Is the irony of light,
A surreptitious score
Where sequins, cufflinks
Add such brilliant grace-notes
As should not be heard

Or seen – no smile
To leap above his shirt-front
Kindling it, no blaze to lure
Her chiffon like a dazzled moth –
This being how they almost
Love each other, no whole flame
But partial glimpses
From the edge of music.

Boat Building Near Flatford Mill, 1815

for Patric Dickinson

In her bottle of English air,
A clouded Suffolk distillation,
She assembles, crafted sturdily
From earth to current crystal.

*

Potion, love-draught, kegged
Essential landscape swelling
To the ring of hammer, hoop and stave
Within an ark of grace and labour.

*

Afloat, her sure return begins
To a dry bed, the skeleton
Capsized, the rib-cage
Held by children as their first redoubt.

A Family Outing

Once more, as if in the back seat,
I'm small and ashamed
And between two aunts. They say
You have prayed for rain. It has rained.
You have spoiled the picnic.

We take a narrow road
Through heather. This is the path
Of righteousness and there will be
No picnic. The rain
Is dear to their hearts.

They say: *We shall tell*
Your father. We shall not
See you again. Small boys
Should always know what they're asking.
God is not mocked . . .

And it still hurts
As if on that same dark journey:
Is this the rain I prayed for,
This my wife, or those my children
In the back seat giving no answer?

Mr Dyer

Close to retirement from
My father's office, founded by
My grandpa. *A. C. Mole & Sons*
Regd. Taunton, Somerset, but not
To know *this* son, not me
Who proudly nominated
Mr Edgar's lad, was treated
Every visit with
A special bar of
Chocolate Cream or Fry's
Five Boys produced
By fiscal prestidigitation
From a safe marked
Current A/cs and glittering
With silver foil as if
He saw the future settled there
Unmelted in my hand.

The Thorn Bush

Now it has offered him one last white flower
And pain is taken here between his fingers.

An immaculate ghost, a token —
He holds an angel up to its own light.

All that has ever hurt is born in this,
The moment of return, the covenant.

We are not a randomness of flakes falling
But this one blossom, always the last.

from

In and Out of the Apple (1984)

Passing

At seventy, my father's life
Instructs me; one lung
Gone, the other — less than itself —
Still gasps with asthma.
There is no end to the end

Which goes on. It is
My own slow death. Like him
I vanish while my two sons
Hug me here, not understanding
Why they do, until

There is nothing between us —
Only, in photographs,
My living arms around them
As I slip invisibly
From theirs.

The Veil

Under the gauze, your mask
Becomes a mould of animation.
Time pours into it
And searches every feature.

An appropriate thought —
Solemn, beyond reproach,
Like a huge lily, waxed to perfection,
Sharing your death.

But this, too — the pantry
Where we hid from bombers,
The pale eggs in waterglass
Safely around us

And there, on the darkest shelf,
One pitcher of precious milk —
I lift it now from its cold place,
Drawing the veil and drinking.

From the Family Album
– Torquay 1948–55

Winter, the Roslin Hall Hotel's
Night Porter, always
Greeted our late arrivals,
Lifting my small suitcase

First from the boot.
True to his name
He never smiled, but that mock salute
Was part of the game

We were all a part of –
It knew what we were –
The guv'nor, his lady wife
And the young sir

Who would soon be the guv'
As if without end,
As if that genteel Father Above
Were a family friend

Who would keep the Hotel in business
With Winter still there –
The eternal, bourgeois, God Bless
Fortnight . . . Oh l'hiver

De mon âge, Winter, you
Salute the world I have always
Known I belong to.
Take my suitcase.

Listening

... each ear
Is listening to its hearing, so none hear.

W. H. Auden

So you play a little, you said. *Well*
Listen to this – Ben Webster's
Tenor, Oscar Peterson, and both of us
Unwinding after yet another
Local reading you'd arranged –
Sheer Poetry! If we'd played them this . . .
Ah yes, if we'd played them this –
Already we were old conspirators –
I smiled back at you, squinting
Through a murky tumbler, your propitiatory
Double-scotch for guests – *I'm sorry*,
Really, about the numbers. They'd probably have been
The same if you were famous. Or even, of course,
If we had played them this . . .

It's the way he breathes. You can hear it.
I could, but then you watched me
Hearing it, you watched
Merely for confirmation just as earlier
You'd heard me read, not hearing
What I had written . . .

Listen, though, you insisted
Can you describe it? There isn't a word.
No, there wasn't, not then
With you expecting it and me
The Visiting Poet, but last night
After nine years I heard the track again
And suddenly I was squinting at you
Through that tumbler, smiling
As I wrote down this . . . I heard
The fugitive gift of tongues,
A halo of resonant air
Around the mouthpiece, the invisible

84

Rhythms pulsing out and out
Towards containment, each
Note a mere particular, the quick
Melodic husk already
Cracked into silence, a freedom beyond wings . . .

Yes, but listen, you say, *all those words, words,
And you still don't hear it.
Even the breath swings.*

Trees at the Frontier

Shrugging great-coats off
They turn their backs on each other,
Rooted in common earth
But not a leaf between them.

Not a bird either.
Too much has tugged here
For the worm of history, so many cold dawns
Stripping down to this . . .

Wind in their poor forked branches
Is a siren's echo, rain
A mother's lament in exile
Under frozen skies,

And one more army
Will not settle the matter—
Like the first leaves of autumn
Its blood spreads at their feet.

They have forgotten the seasons.
They are naked in their shame.
They will have nothing to do with this
Even when spring returns.

Song of the Diplomat

When the Party's losses are the People's gains
You'll find me near the border changing trains.

You'll find me near the border changing trains
When the blood runs free and the free blood stains.

When the blood runs free and the free blood stains
The People's losses are the Party's gains.

When the People's losses are the Party's gains
You'll find me near the border changing trains.

Less Than Sixpence

Now let us educate you, let us, let us . . .
Cracking the crust, this rare politico's
A brave one, a home-baked
Brilliant blackbird, beaked
And gaping far beyond his pastry —
Listen to the facts, now, listen to me . . .
God save the Queen in her parlour,
God save the Counting House forever
And the silver spoon, the gold plate
And all those words which are good enough to eat.
Nobody loves peace more than he does,
Of course, but he'd peck off any nose
To spite her face, poor maid
Alone in the garden with nowhere to hide
When the world ends. It's the *balance*
She doesn't understand, the courtly dance
Of money and power. *Oh listen, listen . . .*
If only she'd hang out reason
With the clothes. Things are not simple;
They are history's manifold example.
You can't just wash them and hope.
Oh keep faith with the faith we keep.
If not for you, for the sake of your children.
Of course we hope it will never happen.
That little white shirt on the line
Which waves at the future, take it in, take it in,
It signals surrender. The skull and bones
Could not be more fatal. *So we come into your homes*
Tonight and tomorrow and tomorrow and tomorrow
Telling you why and when and how
Until you understand. We have baked the pie
And now you'll eat it. Your destiny
Must be to go on listening to reason, its song
Of so much less than sixpence . . .
                                    But no, this is wrong, wrong.
Switch off, walk out in the garden, there's time yet

To hang out a whole wardrobe. Why not?
And remember, a pocket-full of rye is something.
Plant each grain of it, then let the blackbirds sing.

The Bridge

– Van Gogh

From bank to bank beyond, it passes
Either way across a canvas's

Framed window. Two invisible
Distances exchange two groups of people

Running in both directions
On an artful bridge which is no one's

But its painter's. Whatever chance guess
Most pleases you, he knows

Why, for example, the rain fell
At that moment in a blue squall

Making one man in his hurry
Almost dance as if almost merry

Or how that merest twig of a boat
Stayed there, taming the flood

Like a Sunday punt, or even –
After the why and the how – the exact when

Of the storm's completion, its return
To our present tense, to a pattern

Which is neither your own mind's image
Nor these few words on my page

But given, held, and making plain
The bridge between us here inside its frame.

On the Bridge

– a version of Rilke's Pont du Carrousel

Stone-blind and half-way on this bridge of stone
He stands above the river. People glide
Like glittering water past him, open-eyed
But no less fated, just as much alone;
His blank face holds their passing in a frame
And makes a show of what they dare not name.

He is their paradigm, extinction's echo
Echoing itself, a boundary mark
To concentrate their absence in the dark
Which travels with them as they come and go.

Rain

It spills from the brim
Of his black bowler
In Bradford or Halifax
Years before Hitler.

It shines on the listeners'
Umbrellas, on the steps
Of the Railway Hotel,
On the stained moustaches.

It returns the government
To its briar pipes,
To its conscience, to safe seats
Far from the window.

It soaks to the very skin
Those unborn children
Stamping their murderous boots
Down Prospect Alley.

A Sunday Painter

Parking his Citroën between the planes,
He sets an easel up and picks a brush.
Two temperate children play well-ordered games.
His wife reads Camus in a *Livre de Poche*.

He paints till lunch. The colours are discreet;
They wait there on the palette patiently
Until he needs them. One by one they meet
The nice requirements of his cautious eye.

At one o'clock *le déjeuner sur l'herbe* —
The elements compose themselves on cue.
Nothing in nature troubles to disturb
Its proper harmonies of green and blue.

The picnic hamper's little leather straps
Release a galaxy, immaculate,
Which showers domestic silver in their laps
And serves up moonlight on a porcelain plate.

Then, *de rigueur*, a brief, enchanted sleep
For wife and children as the sun resumes
Its gilded station where the painters keep
A space for it on Sunday afternoons.

He touches in a few last details, so —
His time is running out. He cleans the knife.
Ambition more than this was years ago.
He's made a decent compromise with life.

Easel and hamper packed into the car,
They set off home to plan the days ahead.
Monsieur le peintre, how talented you are,
Unique and wholesome as a loaf of bread!

Incident at Snape

The pent rage
Of the Punch and Judy operators,
Him and her
And their fury —

Their rickety, striped booth
Is half-constructed;
It flaps in the flat wind
From the estuary.

Somewhere along the road
They have quarrelled
Coming here, and consequently
Hiss at each other.

He slams down the lid
Of their travelling-box
She opens it again
Again he slams it down.

Glimpse upon glimpse
Of shadowy puppets,
The baby quietly sleeping
With the hangman.

The booth advertises
Theatre of Delights
But here is a far from
Peaceable kingdom.

Already they gather,
The children, suffered
To gape at this enterprise
Of painted rictus,

And now for the show
With its burlesque anger –
The puppets the oldest
And latest thing

While the reeds down-river
Hiss like a Greek Chorus:
*What is coming, children,
Is what you are.*

The Birthday

What did he do? His mother laughed then cried,
His father's silence made the garden cold.
Guilty, perhaps, of being five years old,
He's sent their hurt love terribly inside,
And now a shadow spreads across the grass
From where he sits tight in his pedal car
Gripping its wheel, remorseless avatar
Of what his birth has somehow brought to pass.

He watches as the tall french window keeps
Their dumb-show at a distance in its frame;
They'll never come back to him as they came
Just now before it happened, so he weeps
A little but not much to learn that truth —
Casting its shadow, neither cruel nor kind —
Encroaches on his parents like a blind
Pulled slowly upwards to obscure them both.

Difference

for Patricia Beer

Flattening Crimond at our ironing-board
My aunt would launder linen without end
For the bed she'd come to sleep in, and pretend
Her loneliness was precious to the Lord;
Or *Jesus Loves Me* at the kitchen sink —
A cracked falsetto shrilling round its rim
While distant tables laid themselves for Him,
Immaculate, expectant, on the brink
Of somewhere I could almost recognize
As madness but was always gently told
Was *difference* waiting to be understood
When He had closed those startled, innocent eyes
Whose meaning might come clear if I grew old
Repeating daily: *All God gives is good.*

The Singers

We heard them leave our neighbours and draw nearer,
Easing their rough throats. One had a wicked cough.
Another could hardly have made his purpose clearer—
Give them Noël, collect, and then push off.

But on our doorstep they assumed politeness,
Whispered, fell silent, let the song begin,
And all we had lost was kindled by its brightness
Shrill as heartache, crying to come in.

The Plum Tree

Grandfather's plum tree
Ripened in his garden:
Don't pick them, my boy,
Until they're ready.

His voice was a huge plum
Velvet and purple;
All the good things
Fall into your lap.

But work, work –
You must be ready
For the plum jobs, my boy,
The topmost branches.

He had been a banker –
No beggarman, thief –
He knew the tree
That money grows on.

His smoking-jacket
Was plum-coloured velvet.
So were the curtains
In his wife's front room.

She was Victoria,
Would you believe it?
Victoria Regina
And jam for tea.

Wasp Talk

Dead, but quizzical on my workdesk –
Buzz buzz, poor stripy-coat
In and out of the apple, it is all done.

What I have written I have written.
Oh how we should understand each other,
Marauders of the dying fall.

You eased a passage through sweetness
And are gone. Here on the page
You leave your little lyric sting

As if to say *Was it worth it?*
All that fruitless irritation of the air
Never to come to ripeness until now.

But even as I sweep you to the ground
Your ghost is singing in the pane, a good line
Rescued from its poem. Try again.

Song of the Hat-Raising Doll

I raise my hat
And lower it.
As I unwind
I slow a bit.
This life —
I make a go of it
But tick-tock time
I know of it.

Yes, tick-tock time
I know of it.
I fear the final
O of it,
But making
A brave show of it
I raise my hat
And lower it.

A Different Ending

Standing at the graveside
With a disinterred numbskull,
He finds nothing to say
That has not been said.

But he'll say it again —
A grandiloquent flesh
On the jawbone of language,
Its jowls and its claptrap,

Those resonant names —
Alexander, Caesar —
A rhetoric so easy
And true? Too true.

He speaks of death
And the skull starts nodding:
Now you have it,
Ah now you're talking.

Lie down, lie down,
You must take what's coming.
Compose yourself
For decomposition.

But why should we listen
To this empty-headed
Rattle of wisdom,
This pair of noodles?

Let them alone
With their consolation,
Their rest, their silence,
Their beautiful phrases.

Let all that poetry
Look after itself
And the wind go whistle
Through vacant chambers.

Let us at least
Write a different ending
In such plain speech
That it begs no question.

Let it only say
That a life was lived here
Loved to the limit
And now is not.

from

Homing (1987)

Adder

Walking my own blue hills,
The Quantocks,
I disturb an adder
And remember –

Victory V,
Black V for venom,
Churchill's long cigar,
The hiss of Hitler,

Tongue-flick
In the crackling undergrowth
Of intermittent
Wireless wavebands,

Vy the viper
Couldn't vipe her . . .
Even our riddles
Had a German accent.

Snake in the grass
But not our garden
Where no handkerchief
Would wave surrender,

Herr Leviathan,
The Poisonous One,
Monster of Coils
And vivid markings . . .

In my dream, inside
A Chilprufe sleeping suit,
I killed him nightly
With bare hands.

Coming Home

The son they love came home then went away.
They asked him why he cried out every night.
He didn't tell them and he couldn't stay.
They try to reach him but he'll never write.
They lie together now. They sleep apart
And still, in dreams, each breaks the other's heart.

And still, in dreams, he's haunted by a child
That stood a moment, looked into his eyes
Not guessing just how far he was defiled,
As if his combat-jacket were disguise.
Don't let the little bastards get to you.
You know exactly what you have to do.

All wars are guilty of their own remorse
And have it out with us before they end.
Some may be just, no doubt. Of course.
In time your enemy becomes your friend.
But there are debts the future can't reclaim —
To kill a child and not to know its name.

To kill a child that couldn't run away,
That stood a moment after it was shot
With puzzled human eyes as if to say
Like you I was so why now am I not?
Then fell. He shot the mother too.
It seemed exactly what he had to do.

And then it seemed exactly where to be
Was nowhere where he had to think of home,
The horror of all words meant lovingly,
The ignorant kindness everyone had shown.
Not only nightmares slay the innocent
And that's the reason why he came and went.

And that's the reason why this can't go on,
And why it's almost culpable to write,
And why I can't stop thinking of our son
And of how easily we sleep at night,
How in this house if anybody screams
We joke next morning. It was only dreams.

Oh only dreams that simply come and go,
That tell us nothing that we can't forget.
We lie beside each other snugly, two
Such comfortable, cautious parents, yet
There was a child who came and went away.
They said *We love you* but he could not stay.

The Lost Boy

Mother, oh mother,
Your cupboard's not bare.
I know without looking
The lost boy's in there.

His bones are all shiny.
He's wearing my shoes.
It wasn't his picture
They showed on the News.

Our telephone's ringing.
Why do you just sit
Like a difficult puzzle
The last piece won't fit?

And where is my father?
What have you both done?
Will somebody find me?
Is the lost boy your son?

His footprints are my prints.
There's blood on the floor.
Oh mother, dear mother,
Let me open the door.

Home

They've called it *Remember* –
Near the front gate
A bijou bi-plane spins its propeller
Pipping each post – phut phut –

While its hinged mannikin
Never short of wind
Cranks and cranks the handle
Over, down, and

Up, then breezily over
In endless recall
Which goes on turning forever
Like nothing at all.

Learning the Ropes

Dear Doctor Universe,
Your medicine ball
Is our dream bolus,
A coveted cure-all:
These are the ropes
And we are learning them.

Brisk mats bristle
As expertise should
But you blow your whistle –
No bloody good!
These are the ropes
And we are learning them.

The floor shines so.
It reflects your skill,
The cold walls echo
Overkill! Overkill! –
These are the ropes
And we are learning them.

That high wooden horse
Where you somersault
Resembles a hearse –
It is not your fault.
These are the ropes
And we are learning them.

Parallel bars
Mount, rung by rung,
To extravagant stars
Where your praise is sung:
These are the ropes
And we are learning them.

All your equipment
Is in its place –
Oh betterment, betterment
By disgrace:
These are the ropes
And we are learning them.

Dear Doctor Universe,
Let us pay
For our just deserts
With an apple a day:
These are the ropes
And we are learning them.

The Song of the Pie

It is time to bake our pie.
    The brave beaks clack together,
But look at each beady eye
    As it reckons the price of a feather.

The brave beaks clack together:
    Our recipe must be the best
As it reckons the price of a feather
    And takes good care of your nest.

Our recipe must be the best.
    It offers you dozens of eggs
And takes good care of your nest
    If you stand on your own thin legs.

It offers you dozens of eggs.
    There's a special way to take them.
If you stand on your own thin legs
    You are much less likely to break them.

There's a special way to take them
    That you'll know if you've used eggs before.
You are much less likely to break them
    When you have a few thousand in store.

That you'll know if you've used eggs before
    Is our a priori *assumption.*
When you have a few thousand in store
    You deserve some reward for gumption.

Is our a priori *assumption*
    Unreasonable, do you think?
You deserve some reward for gumption,
    Only the bad eggs stink.

Unreasonable, do you think?
  But why should you make such a fuss?
Only the bad eggs stink.
  All the best eggs vote for us.

But why should you make such a fuss
  When we promise that things will go well?
All the best eggs vote for us.
  They know it's the truth we tell.

When they promise that things will go well
  It is time to bake their pie.
We know it's the truth they tell,
  But look at each beady eye.

Morwenstow

'I would not be forgotten in this land'

R. S. Hawker

Golden commerce
With an insect city
Stalking its colonnades
Of coastal barley.

Be wise, sluggard,
Look to the ant,
The ladybird, the Meadow Brown —
Awake! Awake!

*

Or the bees' prudence
In a high wind:
Each of them picks a pebble up
For steady flight —

Thus Robert Hawker
Teasing Thomas Acland —
Then he drops it, sir,
At the hive's entrance.

*

Too many names now
Crowd the shivered timbers.
Parson Kilroy
You were here and here,

This boxed scriptorium
Your hut of samples —
Not all epitaphs
Are writ on water.

*

Bless the breakers
In the name of all those broken
As our cry comes unto thee
Mon Père! Mon Père!

How shall we know
Our God made manifest?
No fog, no wind, no rain,
No congregation.

*

Orient but mortal
Stepping west,
An opiate blossom
Amongst ripened corn.

Across the sea
A crimson sunset
Sheds its petals
One by one.

*

Come to thy God in time,
Thy Lord at last:
Remote, unfriended,
Melancholy, slow.

A very awful path,
The final journey,
Though the burden of this parish
Was a crucial pain.

*

Catholic, Anglican,
What matter
At the last withdrawing roar
From bone, granite,

To the gold horizon,
To a hive of air
Where every soul comes home
And drops its ballast.

John Wesley Preaching at Gwennap Pit

Here at this depth I am stunned by faith,
Its visitation a small stone dislodged
From the Lord's mountain – that sheer ledge –
Come whispering at first like scree
Then gathered to the resonance of wrath
And veritable hugeness hurled at me.

What else beside the multitudes, my God?
Their hallelujahs, their pale smitten faces
Marvellously thralled, the tumbling innocence of grace
That rolls and roars so playfully to heaven –
Oh strict seizure, madness in my method,
I am all tongues and one thing to all men.

The Gift

So, if it seems
That only
Nowhere's left
Then go there
Willingly.

Let now
Slip through your fingers
Like dry earth,
Let soon
Be your rain-dance.

Between here
And there
The clouds are blossoming.
They wave
On stems of sunlight.

Gather them
Unthinking
In a loving armful
As their gilded burden
Welcomes your return.

Then, though it seem
That only
Nowhere's left
You'll stay here
Willingly.

Answer Phone

Please leave your name.
I shall call you back.
There is no one here.
Do you have a number?

Do you have a cat?
I have four children.
They keep me busy.
They should be back.

I shall call your number.
My mind is empty.
There is no one there.
Please leave my name.

Please leave my cat.
He has no number.
Do you want four children?
They have names.

Please name your children.
My cat is Rover.
He will call you back.
I keep him busy.

The Doll's House

We are not speaking.
I have taken your words
And you mine.
They miss each other
Like homesick children.

I have hidden your words
In the study:
They are *Cooker*,
Washing Machine, Deep-freeze
And *Do you love me?*

You have hidden my words
In the kitchen:
They are *Club*,
Appointment, Handicap
And *Where is my shirt?*

After tonight
We shall probably find them.
If not,
They have lived with us long enough
To find their own way back.

The Station Wife

This is me and Anna
In our masks and combat jackets
On the runway and that's
Gas that yellow you can almost
See the edges and the men
Inside it with their hoses laughing
At how silly we looked they said
And looking just as silly I'd say
Like space-invaders in a field
Of mustard Anna says
We all look silly and we'd
All be dead if this was real
Though if we keep prepared
We won't be which is why
We're practising and anyway
It all looks real enough to me
And even Jacqueline admits
To feeling just a little sexy
Taking us with all those men
Behind us and us sort of
Crouching there like that and
Grinning underneath our masks
But what's so really good's
The definition of the edges
Round that yellow cloud
With all the men inside
And them so blurry even Jacqui's
Pleased with how this one came out.

2

This is Sue and Debbie
On the rifle range I
Took it and that's
Greg and Terry lying there

Beside them straightening
Their aim and swapping wives
Said Terry with his other arm
Round Debbie's shoulder
So what next I wondered as
The rounds of ammo thudded into
Mannikins with bullseyes
Where their parts would be
Then all of us ran up and counted
While the dummies stood there
With their eyes all dead and staring
Like a seizure and the men exclaiming
Well done girlie with their arms
Around the targets' shoulders begging
Take us take us till I laughed
So much I couldn't get it
In and nor can Trevor
Anymore says Anna but I
Wish I had so you could see
The weird resemblances there were
Between those riddled mannikins
And Greg and Terry.

3

This is Tracy standing by the wire
With cutters for a laugh you
Can't tell which side of the fence
She's on but then what happened is
The reason I can't laugh or tell you
What there is to tell since no one told us
Why the siren why the inner gates
Were closed and why our men
Ran criss-cross in the distance then
Assembled on the runway I
Could just see Trevor Greg
And Terry then a tall guard
Snatched my camera saying
Later love you'll get it back
And there's me wondering

What would I do if this was real
Or if it is this time
And where the children are
And must we stay forever with
These skulls this hardware all
The loveless sexiness of being here
Inside the wire outside
The inner gates where even Paul
Goes running criss-cross at
What secret purposes then
Comes home high to hoist his
Penis up and tell me
Baby take a photograph of that.

Toy Bricks

Take two for the man-child
Fury, to be hurled
At a helplessness marked NO
Which is all of your world
And your father's, where nothing is piled
Times nothing into which
Nothing will seem to go.

Build says mother. *Imagine yourself
Inside it.* She has papered the walls
With dinner money. *We are not rich
Like television, but with luck and the school's
Help* . . . On a high shelf
The last baked beans are a balancing trick
Above an empty fridge.

To wake one day to the wolf's
Huff and puff — his jaw
Slavering as he follows you to school.
He knows a house of straw
When he sees one. His impatient face
Is teacher's. You have a toy brick
In each pocket. This is not a good place.

This is not television. Outside,
Real people stamp their feet
Around a brazier, hugging their shoulders —
Take nothing from nothing, divide
By nothing times police and soldiers.
Jack builds his house on *Playschool.*
The wolf waits in the street.

At dinner-break your steaming mash
Has misted the glass. You draw
Two fierce eyes and the familiar jaw,
Take blatant aim and smash

The system. Shameless, you stand there
Rigid, bitter, frowning, without tears.
The splintering chime is music to your ears.

Build said mother. You have not.
She comes for you. She weeps,
Recriminates, but doesn't understand.
Something has hold of you for keeps.
You stride ahead, beyond her, as the gulf
Between you opens, as you take his hand
And walk home with the wolf.

Condemned

I sat next to Dad at breakfast
And we ate a hearty meal
But his face, long as a judge's,
Stared at the family mail
As if looks could kill —

Together we sentenced the world
To life. Our tears were wet.
Mum threw salt over her left shoulder
And put a hard-boiled egg in my pocket
To eat now that I'm older.

The Conjurors

They came and went
At my friends' parties
Always asking us to
Please be of assistance –

To peer up sleeves
And pummel bowlers,
Take a card from somewhere
Near the middle of the pack.

Their jokes were a mystique
The adults laughed at
Like a cloudy rabbit
Hung above our heads.

In stained white
Waiters' gloves, each ghostly finger
Frisked our future
With a shrimp's translucence.

Though we cheered
And cried *Hey Presto!*
All the best games started
After they had gone.

From Doctor Watson's Casebook

The Case of What He Ordered

No, not this afternoon, Holmes, not the violin.
A good read's more the ticket, don't you think?
Not the *Police Gazette* . . . A book you could get lost in,
Foreign climes etc. What? No, not that Chink
With the fingernails – too close to home.
You really must relax. No, absolutely not,
You've read it twice already. Which? *The Moonstone*?
Gracious, old boy, be sensible. Less plot, less plot!

The Case of The Ten Green Bottles

Look, Mrs H, between you and me
And the old five-barred proverbial, as it were,
I'm sure they don't fall accidentally.
They're being pushed. Haven't you noticed since he put them
there
How strangely he's behaved? No, I haven't exactly seen
Him do it, but he's not like himself at all –
Ten bottles, Watson, he told me, *and they must be green*.
A normal chap hangs pictures on the wall.

The Case of The Missing Proverb

Dash it all, Holmes, sometimes you go too far.
This is the wrong tree that you're barking up.
Of course you're a genius, I know you are,
But why can't you ever stop?
Two in the bush, old man? What's that?
Half the time, you know, I just can't understand
A word you say. You're talking through your hat!
One in the . . . One *what*? *Whose* hand?

The Case of The Apologetic Parenthesis

Yes, yes, dear reader, I make
Allowances. Life would be very dull
Without him. No, I can't have my cake
And eat it, but it's pretty awful
When you always get the crumbs *before*
They've fallen from the great man's table
If you see what I mean . . . (I'm a bad hand at metaphor)
And I'm far too agreeable.

The Case of The Amazing Coincidence

Absolutely, Holmes, oh yes, bang
On, old man, you must be right –
What else, indeed, but an orang-outang
Would have left its prints tonight
At just this spot beneath the Major's window?
Yes, I did hear that strangled cry.
Holmes, you've done it, by jingo!
Oh my! Oh my! Oh my! Oh my! Oh my!

The Case of The Remorseless Conjunction

There are times, believe me Lestrade,
When I'm jolly glad of my revolver,
Times when I tell him *Bring in Scotland Yard*
But he won't (of course), when we're knee-deep in heather
On Dartmoor (and gorse) and he hasn't a clue
And he's *loving* it and there's probably quicksand
And a bally hound with luminous fur and I mention you
In passing and he gives me that look and . . .

The Case of The Déjà Vu

Well, Holmes, another handsome lady
Called while you were out – black veil,
Something about a letter, obviously
End of her tether, don't you know. Blackmail.

The usual jitters. So I sat her down
Until she calmed a bit, then she upped and went
Leaving her card (they all do) with an out-of-town
Address. Shall I call a cab? No, this time it's Kent.

The Case of The Fulfilled Wish

Reader, one posthumous account
And then that's that, I promise you.
I've had my bellyful. I can't
Take any more. What am I going to do?
A leaf from Moriarty's book –
I'll lure him to some dangerous high place
Then . . . *Look behind you, Holmes old fellow, look!*
And that will have been our very last last case.

The Impertinence of the Thing

Past forty, a lyricist
Unsung, prone to self-pity
And troubled by the dead
Weight of every
Line, each further from my best,

I think of the young Joyce just
Happening to pass through London
On Yeats's birthday, or
(Was it?) expressly come
To do what must be done

When the time arrives
In all poets' lives
Which was (ie.) to make straight
For the Cavendish where W.B.
Sat ensconced in state

Correcting proofs while sipping
Luke-warm jasmine tea
And not expecting anything
At all like this considering
The eminence of already distinguished *gris*

He might reasonably
Have assumed – Well, Joyce
(Says Oliver Gogarty) knocked on Yeats's door
And in readiness was
Clearing his thin voice

With bat-eyes narrowing
Behind their lenses when
Yeats, his sight already
None too good either, in that familiar sing-
Song called *Come in!*

Then turned to the young blur
Suddenly framed there
And heard *What age are you, sir?*
To which *I'm forty*
He replied, and presumably thought he'd

Appear quite grand, quite mezzo del cammin
To the young fellow who would not come in
But who explained simply
You are too old for me
To help, I bid you goodbye said he

And went, leaving W.B.
(Says Gogarty) *amazed by the impertinence*
Of the thing, but good for Joyce
Say I, sound sense,
And good for the old paycock too

Because there's nothing like a witty
Exchange between the greats
(Bravo Joyce *and* Yeats!)
To reduce a poet's dull self-pity
To absurdity

And so, being older
Than either was then,
Let me laugh now with one
Now the other
And now with both men.

The Circuit

Once more out of this shoe-box
(Christmas accessories) dear tangled friends
With your plaited emerald flex
And familiar chime of chip-chink
Tumbling over my wrist, for the mind's
Ease for a moment I have you to thank

For my father's warm hand resting
Briefly on mine as again together
We number the dead ones and the wrong
Connections, restoring a light
Whose fitful flick and quiver
Is the love we shall celebrate

Tomorrow with the decked tree
Earthed in its yearly circuit
Of recurrence. When I say
Happy Christmas my own ghost
Will shine along the branches, lit
By all that is never lost

Though very soon forgotten. In two weeks
We shall be back here, dulled
And searching for this battered box I take
You from tonight to be, dear tangled friends,
A light of the world
Before the dark descends.

On a Line from Pasternak

Life is not a stroll across a field.
Whatever else it is it isn't that.
And luck is something more than the black cat
Which crossed your path just once when, still a child,
You thought there was no other beast in view—
That pussens sauntered by for none but you.

He didn't. Not a whisker left to chance
The necessary journey that he took
Out of his picture in your story book
To where your own son's wilful innocence
Finds and returns him, still beguiled
By life that seems a stroll across a field.

The Cost

Let this poem step
From its own perfection
And words be themselves again
In sweet disorder —
An undressed language,
A simple purpose
Like the child's tyrannical
Me! Me! Me!

But that little face
Is of deprivation,
A stone, a cloud
Or a flower, autonomous,
Plucking its petals
One by one.

from

Depending on the Light (1993)

The Cherry Tree

Welcome to the cherry,
So unequivocal,
So full
Of itself, so utterly

Not you, not me, with our same
Questions,
The old stones'
Word game

Of this year
Last year
Next year
Never . . .

Of *Do you love me*
As much as. . . ?
Or *Who was*
He or she?

Or *Do you love me less*
Than I love you?
Or *Tell me something new.*
Haven't I heard this?

Welcome to the cherry,
Its white silence,
Its common sense,
Its letting be.

The Falling Man

And finally the act
We'd waited for,
Our own inimitable
Falling Man

Who climbed his pyramid
Of chairs and tables
With a whimper
And a sheepish grin

Until, so nearly there,
He cried out, leaping
From a crumpled clatter
Clear into the stalls

Where all of us
Applauded, rushed to be
The one who set him on his feet
And brushed him down

While brisk assistants
Rearranged the stage,
Rebuilt the whole construction
Higher still, more skeletal,

And so, prepared,
He turned again to bow
Then set off warmed
By fresh applause

Which chilled to silence
As he neared the top
And this time
Would he by a whisker

Make it? No,
But as he fell
How irreversibly his mirth
Became our guilt

And as he lay there
In that wooden cage
Collapsed around him
Laughing, laughing

At our laughter,
It was you that cried out
Look, The Falling Man has fallen,
Help him. Help!

Travellers

The pin-striped thug, the middle-aged
Sartorial bully is a lost soul
In this tunnel. Tense, ophthalmic
On the edge of murder, going
Nowhere between stations. Opposite
I read a book and then pretend to, watching
As his anger swells from silence,
Pours into a well that can't contain it
And the black bile overflows. A girl
Sits down beside him opening her bag
And taking out three carrots. She begins
To bite them – click, click, click, click –
As if he wasn't there, as if beside her
Was a gentleman who wouldn't mind
Because he was a gentleman, at most
Might be amused by this – click, click –
Or say *My little rabbit*, but instead
His sour face swivels round towards her
Muttering *More noise, come on, please
Make more noise, why not, let's hear it,
We all want to hear it!* He attempts
A supercilious snarl. Her pale face
Pales still further but her eyes are tip-toe
On the edge of murder. She outfaces him,
She blinks, she bites again – click, click –
And gazes coldly. She will never be
His victim but again he tries. *If you don't
Stop I'll pull the communication cord
And then you'll have to and that won't
Be all* – click, click, click, click,
She finishes. She reaches for another. *Do
She says then you'll be fined* – click, click –
Until he sits there speechless and until
I close my book. The train slows down. She says
I think there's something wrong with you . . .
I leave at the next station.

The Edward Lear Poem

He kept his wife in a box he did
And she never complained though the neighbours did
Because of the size of the box and the way
He tried to behave in a neighbourly way
But smiled too much of a satisfied smile
For a body to know what to make of his smile.

Then there came such a terrible cry one night
Of the kind you don't like to hear in the night
Though the silence that followed was broken at last
By the blows of a hammer which seemed to last
For ever and ever and ever and ever
And no-one set eyes on that man again ever.

La Jeunesse

Straight from her door
Through rows of vines towards
The river, one white bucket
Swinging for Sunday, the air
Fleshed out with heat
So plump this risen morning
Purpling to ripeness
But not yet, but not quite
Yet among these sunflowers
Leaning their weary faces
Huge and vacant
After her, so stooped
So nodding, and the one
Note tolling distantly
Across the river *mort*
La mort comme ça aussi la mort
From the little church's
Bell tower on a low hill
Rising from the vines
And ringing, swinging
Its one black upturned
Bucket emptying
All gathered sound this morning
Everywhere *la vie la mort*
Although she has turned already
Walking to her door.

The Settlement

Steam from an electric kettle
Shrouds its click, then
Two cerulean mugs across the lawn
This droughty summer
Come as a libation
Weighted, brimming, answering
The love which reaches
Out for them, still reaching
For the girl who held them
Balanced just the same
Though in a greener garden
Twenty years ago, held now
Against their soon becoming
Shards discovered in a dry bed
Dusted over.

Shrouded too
But by blue dazzle, light years
From such thoughts as these,
Imperious, perching
On the terra-cotta chimney
Rising from gold thatch,
A gull there briefly
Lifts its Roman head.

The Honesty Box

Bolt upright, seated in a ring
They played the game again
Like ancient children. Not a sound,
No music, not the rustling
Of tissue, nothing that began
Or seemed that it could ever
Stop. And so the box came round
As it had always done, a heavy-hearted
Dull exchange, a passing-on
Of what was neither grief
Nor fear nor hope but only
Mere deception. Some
Gazed blankly at it, some
Were rid of it without a glance
And just a few occasionally
Held it up to listen, hearing
Locked inside the key
Which might have opened it at last,
A distant rattle.

                Then, as they
Shifted it like this from lap
To lap, the miracle occurred. Some
Smiled a little and some wept,
Each cautious, quivering lip
A voice which in another world
Was coming clean, no longer
Guilty of its secret, opening
What one by one these held
In common yet had never spoken of
Until this moment when it seemed
A huge lid lifted from the room
Releasing kindness like a breath
Of sandalwood, so suddenly, so
Sweetly from this box they'd all
Been lost in, as their vision
Gave them to each other, as the key
Turned once in silence and was gone.

A Different Dream

Here is the place for them, the fathers
Who were children, in this clearing
Ringed with cypresses, a garden
Where their love of it can cut the grass
Forever, and the house we all remember
Casts no shadow on the lawn. It's here
In a dream I meet with mine again, his sleeves
Rolled up for the honest work
Just asking to be done. He says
I'll need some help. His tie
Is tucked inside his waist-band, braces
Tight and at the ready. Go!
I walk beside him with a little barrow
As my mother watches us a while
And then goes in. This is the place for us
Until the light starts fading:
Cold my father says *It's turning cold* —
We look up, and a cloud is hanging there
Above the cypresses. We're in
A different dream, a darker.

Now we stand beside each other, loving, lost
And very tired. He says
We've done it, leaning on the mower
At our completed lawn's
Far edge. He calls my mother — *Mother!* —
But she doesn't hear him, no,
Not even as he snaps his braces
In the slack and stoop of weariness.
By now she's reading the illuminated text
Of sunset from a western window
In her empty house: 'God blesses
Those who bless themselves
And then it's over.' This is her love's
Last frame. I'm caught inside it calling
Father! as I run to him again

Across the lawn, beyond my life,
My wife, our children, yes,
For a moment as the two of us
Look once towards the house
Then disappear between the cypresses.

The Walking Bell

after Goethe

Once there was a Sunday child
Who would not go to church,
Who ran into a sunlit field
As far as he could reach.

His mother warned him *Hear the bell!*
You must not make it wait.
Unless you heed the good Lord's call
That bell will seek you out.

No! cried the Sunday child, *Not so,*
It cannot leave its tower.
So off without a care he flew.
He'd darken no priest's door.

And now the bell no longer tolled.
So much for mother's tales.
But what was this? The Sunday child
Turned on his troubled heels.

The bell was chasing after him,
An angry, brazen dome,
It waddled like that scourge of sin
The pastor, crying *Come,*

There's no escape for Sunday's child,
For mother's boy, for you.
You shall forget your sunlit field.
God has decreed it so.

On pumping, pious little legs
With the walking bell behind him,
Torn by briars and lashed by twigs,
The Sunday child ran blindly

Where mother and the pastor stood
To greet him at the porch
And, flanking him on either side,
Escort him into church.

So now, they say, the child is whole
Who'd sickened in the sun
But every time he hears the bell
Virtue goes out of him

And though one stroke, one stroke alone
Can bring him to his knees,
He still recalls the light that shone
Once in a field of praise.

The Carolling Bull

Beware, beware the carolling bull
With its gate wide open, oh three bags full
And over the moon, sing high, sing low,
Sing *Dulce, in dulci jubilo*
With a ring through its nose, a roar in its heart
For everything that's about to start
All over again and again and again
For the little boy who lives down the lane,
Who sleeps on straw then stirs and cries
And remembers how once before his eyes
The stable door burst open wide
As, full of a rush of headlong pride,
It thundered out, the carolling bull,
By Jove, by Jehovah, a holy fool
High on an overdose of joy
And love and rage for its own sweet boy
Who had woken from a dream of peace
To weep at this terrible release,
This sudden, glorious weight of a world
Which would not grow wise but simply old
In a field of praise, still standing there,
The carolling bull, beware, beware.

Passing the Parcel

While the music was playing she passed him the parcel
And he passed it back to her slowly at first
As if guessing its weight or perhaps just admiring
The shop-window gloss of its polka-dot wrapping
But faster then faster they thrust it between them
Away and away like a short-fused explosive

Until it was there in his hands and no music
Which meant that he had to begin to unwrap it
By layer and layer and layer and layer
But he took his time and she wasn't watching
As if they had somehow decided already
The party was over and nothing was in it.

No Answer

They watched his indiscretion
Then arrested him.

They will not name it,
What he did.

With just six words
They broke him —

In their report they wrote
We stood at a respectable distance.

What is a life
According to that measurement?

How far the distance
Worthy of respect.

Item

She left it in the long grass
Bedded there, lullay lullay,
And started walking, anywhere, away
Across a world of darkness to the edge

Then stopped forever, come what may
Of any reckoning. What came to pass
Was boots and tracker dogs, a village
Briefly on the news, the interviews

With nobody who loved her
But must say so anyway, much outrage,
Not a little pity, and rejoicing
For the child found sleeping where it lay.

The Waking

Nothing, it seems, not crowded out
By war, and in my sleep
Its rumours, pad-foot, prowling
Through the darkness dreams
Are guilty of, as if each touch
Were breaking sanctions, love
Reported somewhere culpable
In snow or sandstorm, ambushed
And arraigned with you
Beside me as we walk there
In whatever place is sacred to
The guilt of happiness
Towards a daybreak smeared
Across the blank horizon
Of a barred world, curtainless
And shadowing our bed.

Yet still, without shame,
A place for this, the waking
To familiar warmth, the slow
Shift over of your body
To the groove my rising's
Left for it, the loosed
Indulgent yawn along
The length of you, and arms
Stretched up beyond the headboard
With a little moan, a sensual
Smile by Rembrandt or Vermeer
Or, should you choose, Matisse
Depending on the light
And then the coffee waiting
And the first cars
Coughing in the street.

The Installation

En route for coastal
Sea and sand,
Do we dream
This hinterland

Where cordoned-off
And disenchanted,
A curious garden
Has been planted?

Though it lies here
In the light
Everything seems
Dead of night.

Someone guards
A little hut
Whose door is barred
And windows shut.

Mottled cars
Speed to and fro
On runways
Where we must not go.

Revolving turrets'
Moony plates
Protect a world
Which waits and waits.

A skull-and-crossbones
On live wire
Proclaims its voltage
Like desire.

A lonely golfer
Plays his shot,
Making the place
Seem what it's not.

An innocent
Ballistic sphere
Leaps from the dust
To disappear.

At the crash gates
Men with guns
Scuff their boots
And bite their thumbs

While, troubled by
The watch they keep,
We neither wake
Nor dare to sleep.

Land's End

Now, having reached this point,
What is it? Rocks,
Rocks, rocks, rocks,
The sea's ambiguous answer.

The Point

was not where it went
but where it led him,
how he found it
in the music, out of it
and back, each chorus
risking more, the changes
unrepeatable, already
way beyond transcription
like his wide-mouthed
braying laughter, bracelet
slung on each wrist, percussive
signet fingers, then
that grin and all he'd
ever tell them: *Sure it's dangerous*
and when you see me smiling
you know I'm lost.

Stan Laurel

Ollie gone, the heavyweight
Balletic chump, and now
His turn to bow out, courteous,
A perfect gentleman who
Tips his hat to the nurse

Or would, that is, if he were
Still in business. She
Adjusts his pillow, smooths
The sheets until their crisp-
And-even snow-white starchiness

Becomes his cue. It's time
For one last gag, the stand-up
Drip-feed: *Sister,*
Let me tell you this,
I wish I was skiing,

And she, immaculately cornered
For the punch-line: *Really,*
Mr. Laurel, do you ski? A chuckle –
No, but I'd rather I was doing
That than this,

Than facing death, the one
Fine mess he's gotten into
That he can't get out of
Though a nurse's helpless laughter
Is the last he hears.

Dream Girl

I was the girl who wrote to Noël Coward,
Dated Errol Flynn and Edward G.,
Stiffened her upper lip for Leslie Howard,
Brought Clark Gable down on bended knee,
Drove around the block with Fred MacMurray,
Rode the Ferris Wheel with Orson Welles,
Told the Hays Committee not to worry,
Promised Walter Pidgeon wedding bells,
Followed Bogey's hat down every mean street,
Shared Paul Henreid's last two cigarettes,
Tried in vain to fathom Sidney Greenstreet,
Settled George Raft's hash by placing bets . . .
I was the girl who nearly lost her head
But fell asleep and married you instead.

The Floral Costumier

Open his scented
Wardrobe, find
The little silken
Arum lilies.

From their green
Hangers they
Drift towards you
Blowing kisses.

Theirs is the soft
Sift of a nightdress
In its snowfall
To your ankles

Or the sweetness
Rising, moist
And downy between
Lip and lip.

They are his fingers'
Dream of nakedness
Made flesh,
An incarnation

Of their touch
From root to blossom,
Love's amazement
And a perfect fit.

The Safe Nursery

Never to touch the gold key on the mantelpiece
Never to sharpen a sweet tooth for gingerbread
Never to fall for a promise of palaces
Never to bite on a waxed apple's shininess
Never to tangle with overgrown undergrowth
Never to trust that a beast will negotiate

Always to sniff at the meal put in front of you
Always to listen with caution to grandmother
Always to count up the guests at a Christening
Always to walk out on talkative animals
Always to steer clear of picturesque cottages
Always to make your own bed and then lie on it

The Christmas Angel

Spy of a special branch,
The Christmas angel
Weighs his intelligence
And finds it wanting.

He can scarcely believe
What the little birds tell him
Of an open secret
Not to be kept,

Of love's round-robin
Sealed and delivered
To every doorstep
By a child's pierced hand.

So he spreads the word —
As if, as if —
Like a hush-hush cradle
Rocked in its tree.

Not About Roses

to Mary

I have never written
A poem about roses,
Supposing them
The thorniest subject —

How many before me
Have pricked their fingers
On what they thought
Was the only flower,

The one for love
Without really trying
Like the easiest word
To understand

Or a rhyme so exact
It would live for ever
In its cut-glass bowl
And not need water.

Harder than that
To say *I love you*
With the words still earthed
In a dusty soil

Which nevertheless
Is best for sunflowers
Though too dry for me
To do you justice

Or offer more
Than the curious drift
Of a loving poem
Not about roses.

Sketching the Tortoise

Sketching the tortoise
Should be easy, eye

To unblinking eye
With post-diluvian pencilled

Fingers, but it isn't, shifting
Ceaselessly like

Wind through grass or
Fidgeting those

Little eucalyptus leaves
From light to shade

To light, so slight
You scarcely notice what

It's up to, what
It almost tells us

Not of ourselves alone
But of imagination's

Origins, the slowness
Of a patient world

Revealed by everything
Which won't keep still.

Going On

Scotch and water, warm,
Medicinal, two tablets
On a little tray, his *Times*
Tucked underarm, a dignified
But frail ascent, prolonged
Undressing measured out
By heavy footsteps, coughing
Gently not to worry us, as if
A mere polite reminder, then
The silence of the grave.

And why must I recall this now
As half-way up the stairs
I hear my grown son calling
Going on, then, Dad?
An early night? Sleep well.

New Poems

Points of Departure

The Heart of the Matter

She stood on their spaciously lawn-mowered runway
To watch the first flight of that balsa-wood biplane
He'd known from the start would be long in the making
But worth it for every meticulous moment
Of perspex and dope and the overnight drying
That tightened a wing tip or bedded the cockpit.

And since there was only this one way of learning
She loved him the more for what now had to happen,
His eagerness tangling with over-wound rubber
Which stuttered and thumped into silence and nosedive
Sending him straight as a heart-homing arrow
To weep at her feet in a shortfall of failure.

Beatrix Potter writes the D.H. Lawrence Poem

A bundle of nerves to the tip of his whiskers
Like poor Peter Rabbit he always heard noises
Which punished his dreams long before he allowed them
To hint at a garden where things could be different,
Where stones might be thrown but which didn't break
                                                    windows
And he could leap out of his little blue jacket.

Brought up by mother who told him what not to
And father who slammed doors then went off and did it
In hobnails and moleskins like Mr. McGregor,
He kept to his patch where he listened and listened
To rain on the leaves and a lifetime of echoes
Which chimed at the core of his splintering heartache.

Easy when you Know How

Whatever it was the solution was always
To put a brave face on and try to be ready
Remembering too that it might never happen
Though clearly it had while he hadn't been watching
And as for those stars he'd been taught to call lucky
He couldn't see why he should thank them for nothing.

But oh how they winked up above at each other
Like elders and betters intent on improving
This fierce little innocent monster ingratitude
Breaking his will on the wheel of misfortune
Until he had learnt that all good little sandboys
Were happy as Larry and said they were grateful.

John Betjeman writes the William Blake Poem

Stamping his lace-ups on resonant iron
He climbed the first bridge in the world and then waited
A little god swaddled in suitable clothes
For the smut-flecking fall-out, the moist Empyrean,
And waited and waited until a gaunt signal blade
Rang out the chop-down and thrilled him with clangour.

Then thundering through came the *Cornish Riviera*
To pass right beneath and to shake the foundation
To offer one glimpse in the flash of its passing
Of *King George the Fifth* with its gold bell and buffers
Before he was left there transfigured, translated,
A fiend in the cloud of his fierce adoration.

The Final Chapter

Reader she married him straight up no kidding
And off they both rode on a horse out of Tennyson
(*Exit dactylic with cantering hoofbeats*)
Down splendid perspectives from here to the echo of
Property Property Property Property
Playing their tune although neither was musical.

Wrapped in his silver-lined cloak of assurance
And gripped to the hilt by a circumspect mortgage
He posed for the portrait his status demanded
With her there beside him his hand on her shoulder
As if there could never be discord between them
No terminal weeping or cry from the attic.

Has the Prisoner anything to Say?

From his dead father's wardrobe nothing would fit him,
The pantaloon trousers, the Brobdingnag jackets,
The unopened shirts in their cellophane wrappers,
The neatly-boxed shoes that his feet would get lost in,
And all adding up to a mortal reproach
In the polished mahogany vault of the tallboy.

But what of that other reproach of the small boy
Who found himself guilty of all he'd grown out of,
The snake-belted shorts and the ribbed V-necked sweaters,
The Aertex vests with their Cash's name-tapes?
So judgement seemed passed by the dead twice over
And when that cap fits you must grin and wear it.

A Browning Version

Just with a handful of silver she left him
And caught the next boat-train from London to Dover
Where he (that's the other) had said he would meet her
Then all would be oh such a dream of plain sailing
Through sunlight and breeze and the buffeted sea-gulls
With duty-free perfume and love all the way.

No it didn't work out and to cut a long story
She swallowed her pride and a cold cappuccino
Decided his kind was a probable handful
So better to press on regardless through customs
Where the ribbon she wore in her coat was admired
By a poet booked in on the cross-channel ferry.

The Narrow Escape

He couldn't believe that thirteen was unlucky
Or flick the spilt table salt over his shoulder
Or spit when he spotted a singular magpie
Or bypass a step-ladder's trinity triangle
Sure beyond doubt that the Good Lord had made him
To walk in straight lines by the strict light of reason

Nor did he know how to handle her nonsense
Of moonglow and star signs and vague intuition
Although he could see she was clearly on offer
And lovely and certain to prove worth the taking
So risking a smile like a crack in a mirror
He counted to twelve before closing his diary.

Goodbye to the Suits

Saying goodbye to the suits wasn't easy
So handsome they'd hung on his absence beside her
With spotted silk handkerchief fluffed to a soufflé
And sleeves tapered down to the Midas-touch cufflinks
Which peeped from his wrists on the shirts she'd kept pressing
Like new-minted coins to be snapped up by Charon.

Already she knew he'd gone far on his journey
Which made her accessory after the fiction
That they were a couple success couldn't alter
Or love would abandon but oh he'd become
Such a beautiful shade that reversing their story
Eurydice wept when she opened his wardrobe.

Gone with the Wind

Only by habit she opened her window
To listen for snatches of New Year's Eve carillon
Blocked by a gust and then breezily drifting
Like news of a promise that someone had broken
Although in the distance each luminous church tower
Resounded with hope for a radiant future.

Oh come all good people! was what they were calling
Those bells which once gathered harmonious circles
Of fragile acquaintance that piecemeal had vanished
And left her to doubt whether more could be taken
By what she already was eager to welcome
But knew like a good little girl she must wait for.

Everything in the Garden

She left him in what had become of their garden
With everything leisurely, punctual and patient,
The barrow up-ended, the roller akimbo
And pain potted out into orderly earthenware
Warm to the touch and most precious at sundown
When oblivion had drunk all it could of his day.

Then time to go in for The News and the chat-shows,
The tins that he'd never quite learned how to open,
The mis-matching articles draped over chair-backs,
The shifting of night into place for tomorrow,
The bitter reproach of the photograph album,
The unanswered letters and sleeping alone.

*   *   *

Neither of them Spoke

Neither of them spoke or ever dreamed
This was the last they were to see of him

Who didn't wind the window down
Or wave or even turn his head

But leant a little forward, showed
His new watch to the driver, sat back

Smiling (no, how could he?) to himself,
An unslung satchel cradled on his lap

With diary, pencil case and playing cards
Strapped in and tightly buckled, then

The car drove off, and still
He would not turn, but neither said a word

Because it wasn't done, though later
(Three weeks into term to be exact)

His mother gripped the telephone, cried out
And tried to speak, her husband

Leaning forward, holding her,
A firm hand on each shoulder as she sat back

Rigid in the chair, not even turning
As he went to close the door to be alone together.

The Field

Whoever he was
he stepped into the field
and stood there. Cattle
neither raised their heads
nor shifted, nor
despite the grassy path
that crossed him did he think
to follow it. Whatever
light might be
had gathered watchful
at the rim, and under him
was darkness pressing down
and deepening. The oak
which stood there too
because the scene required it
almost brought him back
to how before he'd come
he might have pictured this,
but still he could not
puzzle out its branches
or the roots which spread
towards him now, and worse
was something distant
much like thunder, voicing
everything, which hung around
and would not leave the valley.

A Native of the Dream

So at home she was, a native
of the dream which started up
around her, creature-world
already wonderful, such hunger
for its language, how to learn
of nature as it must have been
before he named it.

Then his rage,
the search for just one word
which might return them
to become the source of all things
left unspoken, tongues
unloosed by exile into sorrow's
utterance, the pillow-talk
last thing before another dream
of walking in a garden
dumbstruck, utterly alone.

Recurrent

Walking through a narrow pass
where silence from both sides
comes pressing in and only darkness
lies ahead, I know for an instant
(every time more certain) how it is
to be alone, to hear the ocean
loosening its tongue behind me
in unfathomable speech, an echo
of that promise made by both of us
beneath a steep, unbroken sky
when all was sunlight, then
once more we wake from this
together, reaching for assurance
as my dream begins receding
and you fear to tell me yours.

Three Photographs

This one of them
at the start of it, confetti
vague as interference
on a freeze-frame, hats
held halfway off each head
against the bitter wind.

This one later by
twelve anniversaries, already
past the best of it,
dead centre on a bridge
in Scotland, leaning over,
looking down.

This one taken
for the sake of it, which
could be anywhere
or any time of day,
a stretch of water,
railings, and the car.

'Anything but a dull cruise on a level lake'

Anything? I can think of worse.
Drowning, for instance
and not metaphorically,
to leap from starboard after
long deliberation, all those voices
calling from the tongue-tipped waves,
or in the dead of winter
not expecting ice to break your fall
and every bone, when all
you reckoned was the gesture
of a brief immersion
suddenly, like love or something.

Of course, it wouldn't do
to thank your lucky stars
for glassy stillness, for the gift
of your reflection, no
you must be whipping up a storm
to be remembered by,
already bailing water from
a leaky skiff
and making metaphors
about the tatters of its sail,
the cut of cloth against
all odds etc., and how
the rest of us know nothing,
day by little day,
of suffering, who have not even
cast off from the shore.

The Astrakhan

It was one thing
to wrap the astrakhan
about your person,
strutting out as if
all verse that had ever been
depended on a coat
of such expensive cut
that no one meeting you
would dare recall
the enterprise of going naked.

Quite another, though,
to drape it on a chair
then find your cat
asleep there in the lamplight
when you'd finished
writing, take a pair
of scissors, cut around
that shape as if all love
depended on it, leave
her purring on a patch
of most expensive cloth
and wear your coat again
without a second thought.

The Cart

His father made it
while he watched the making,
as the sawdust thickened
on his polished boots

and as the plane went sliding,
pushed two-handed
until golden ringlets
grew from curls,

as planks were laid
and flatly hammered
nail by nail removed
from tightened lips,

as in each hub
the spokes were bedded
and the plated curves
became a rim.

He watched and wondered
at his father's apron,
at its laden pouch,
its cross-hatched leather,

standing his ground
where manhood's magic
wore a cloak like this
and truth was crafted.

For Company

It was always the horizon
his binoculars were trained on,
sweeping it with dips
and inclinations to what end
took time to learn, recalls
a memory I can't let go.

The pair of us, grey socks
inside our sandals, shorts
below our knees, and one foot
on the sea-front railing, steadying
our aim, my pocket-telescope
for company, unfocused

in the shadow of his
concentrated gaze, Horatio
and Hardy out on deck
awaiting action. Now
the enemy is mine, and mine
the child beside me summoning

this snapshot of my father
from his numbered days,
the dark ship there already
clear on the horizon
which I once mistook for distance
and a life ahead.

Beyond Appearance

Always polishing it up
you sit here
shifting this
and that. *Almost*
you say *I'm almost
ready*. It's the same
look in your eyes
as yesterday, a tin-foil
substitute, a trick
to catch the light
as if deception
took a shine
to promises
and was itself
deceived.

And me? I'll come
tomorrow, find you
looking as you
look today, beyond
appearance. *Ready yet?*
I'll ask *Not quite*
you'll say. And in this room
they've brought us to
again you'll sit here
at the table shaping air
between us, shifting
this and that
invisibly until
it shines.

The Balance

Everything at the tip
of itself, the top
of the world, alighting
like this sparrow
on a budding
limb of the forsythia
which bends to a passing
splay-foot touch, a tiny
grip on symmetry
disturbing it, then
weighs its burden in
the balance, held
between retention
and the feathered air.

The Memory of Gardens

Glazed pots after a storm
and water's underhang
on black wrought-iron arm rests
threaded with convolvulus,
the window-frames
recriprocally white, their
lucent-beaded latticing
a jewelled absence, yours
and mine, two faces
pressed against the years
between us looking out
then in to where we lay together
listening to rain, unclouded
by the memory of gardens
we were born to leave.